The Birth of Scotland

POST-ROMAN Alba, the country north of Hadrian's Wall, was divided among four groups. Three of these – the Picts, the Scots and the Britons – were of Celtic origin. The fourth group, the Angles, who settled in the Lothians, were part of the savage 5th-century Teutonic invasion of Britain that scattered the native Britons into Strathclyde, Wales and Cornwall. For Alba, the immediate future was to be in the hands of the Picts and the Scots.

THE SCOTS ARRIVE IN ALBA

The Scots migrated to Alba from Northern Ireland, establishing a colony in and around Argyllshire called Dalriada after their mother country in Antrim. They adapted well to their new environment, and around the year 500 Fergus Mor set up a new dynasty in Dalriada, with its capital at Dunadd. The ambitious Scots now took steps to extend their influence, and when Fergus and his brothers divided Dalriada among themselves, the first tribes were formed: Cinel Lorn, Cinel Garran, Cinel Angus and, later, Cinel Comgall.

THE SCOTS AND PICTS UNITE

Towards the end of the 8th century, the Norsemen from Scandinavia began to attack the Northern coast and islands of Alba, transforming for ever the character of the Hebrides, the Orkneys and the Shetlands. The sustained pressure of the Norse raids on the mainland exhausted the strength of the Picts, and they were unable to resist a claim to the Pictish throne made in 843 by Kenneth MacAlpin, the king of the Dalriadic Scots. His triumphant coronation as king of both the Scots and the Picts took place at the Pictish sacred centre of Scone.

ABOVE: *A replica of the coronation stone of Scone on the Moot Hill at Scone Palace, where Scottish kings were crowned. The original stone was taken to Westminster Abbey in 1297 by Edward I, and only returned to Scotland in 1996.*

RIGHT: *Glamis Castle, the historic home of the Earls of Strathmore and Kinghorne. King Malcolm II died at Glamis after being wounded in battle nearby in 1034.*

RIGHT: The Irish Scot Columba came to Alba in 563, and established a small monastery on the tiny island of Iona. He gradually persuaded the pagan Picts to renounce their Druidic beliefs and embrace Christianity.

THE CELTS AND THE SAXONS

In 1018 the Celtic king, Malcolm II, brought the Lothians under Scottish rule, and in 1034 his grandson, Duncan, became king of a geographically united Scotland. In 1040 Duncan was killed in battle by Macbeth, who was killed in turn by Duncan's son, Malcolm, in 1058.

Malcolm III initiated the antagonism that was to grow between clans and crown. He lived in the Anglo-Saxon Lothians rather than the Celtic north, choosing to move his court to Dunfermline a few years after his coronation at Scone in 1058.

Anxious to consolidate his territory, Malcolm took as his second wife a Saxon, the beautiful and deeply pious Princess Margaret, sister of Edgar the Atheling. He substituted Saxon for Gaelic as the court language; he tried to introduce Roman Catholic beliefs to the Celtic clergy; and he brought feudalism to Celtic Scotland.

BELOW RIGHT: A detail of the Aberlemno Cross Slab, showing a late 7th-century Pictish warrior. The Scots' gradual conquest of the Picts finally ended in their union under the Scottish king Kenneth MacAlpin at his coronation in 843.

Clan versus Crown

UNDER the clan ideal, the land was held communally and administered by the chief; but under feudalism, all land was royal land. The loyalty of the clansmen was that of kinsmen to their chief, not subjects to their king. The determination of successive kings to replace clannishness with feudalism drove a wedge between the Celtic Highlands and the Saxon Lowlands.

BELOW: *For centuries, the impenetrable Scottish mountains protected clansmen from the Crown, both Scottish and English, and from each other.*

SETTLING THE LAND

Not surprisingly, the Scottish kings found it difficult to assert their authority over people living in a remote and inaccessible land. The deep glens surrounded by mountains were gradually settled by the clans: the Campbells in mid-Argyll, the Camerons in Lochaber, the Robertsons in Rannoch, the Mackays in Sutherland. Islands, too, attracted the great families: the MacDonalds in Islay, the Macleans in Mull, Tiree and Coll, with Skye shared by MacDonalds, MacLeods and Mackinnons.

A DETERMINATION TO SURVIVE

Despite the poor soil, the clans attempted to be self-sufficient, living off the small cattle that somehow managed to survive the mountains. In the islands and on the coast the clansmen caught fish and exported their surplus to the Lowlands. In the glens they grew barley for fermenting whisky and oats for making bread. It was a harsh way of life, yet the need to protect their cattle taught these Celtic hillsmen great endurance and military skill. In time, their impetuosity in battle would startle Lowlander and Englishman alike.

ABOVE: *The island of Harris in the Western Isles, held by Clan MacLeod.*

SOMERLED, KING OF THE ISLES

In the mid-12th century, a powerful figure emerged who would set the scene for the clans' battle for autonomy. Somerled was an outstanding warrior of mixed Pictish and Norse blood who, after a ferocious sea battle, won the Kingship of Man from the Norwegians. Now in control of all the Western Isles from Bute to Ardnamurchan, Somerled gave a promise of fidelity to Malcolm IV in return for recognition of his conquests. It was Malcolm's view that Somerled held his lands directly from the crown – but Somerled regarded himself as King of the Isles.

A BID FOR INDEPENDENCE

In 1164 Somerled, determined to demonstrate his defiance of the crown, sailed up the Clyde with a fleet of 150 ships, and sacked Glasgow. At Renfrew, however, he encountered the Steward of Scotland's army, and was killed. But his death was not in vain, for his assertions of independence before the crown set a precedent that would later be emulated by his descendants – the MacDonalds, Lords of the Isles.

Scottish Heroes

In 1297, William Wallace's resounding victory at Stirling Bridge came as a shock to the English and Edward I, who had deposed the Scottish king John Balliol, but this victory was short-lived; the following year Wallace's force was defeated by a vengeful Edward, and in 1305 he was executed. It was Wallace's successor as guardian of the kingdom, Robert the Bruce, who would be crowned king of Scotland and win independence for Scotland, defeating Edward II at the Battle of Bannockburn in 1314.

Clan Structure

Chief
supreme lawgiver

Tanist
nominated by chief (tanistry was a system of succession by a previously elected member of the family)

Commander
military leader

Chieftains
heads of branches of the clan, appointed if chief old or infirm

Gentlemen
claimed blood connection with chief

Clansmen
the greatest in numbers, who were manual workers in peacetime and fighters in wartime

The clansmen accepted the hierarchy without resentment, and were proud to be connected to their chief and to each other. Children (including the chief's) were exchanged among different families within the clan, so that responsibility for their upbringing was shared at all levels.

Clan versus Clan

WHILE many clans were united in opposing the crown, this did not necessarily mean they were at one with each other. Scotland was a land where clan fought against clan, and the crown despaired of securing their loyalty. Divisions within clan groupings were the rule rather than the exception, and sometimes reached a painful conclusion.

ABOVE: *Kilchurn Castle on Loch Awe, home of the Campbells of Glenorchy, who ruthlessly manipulated the feudal system to extend their lands.*

THE BATTLE OF INVERHAVON, 1370

After a particularly vindictive cattle raid on their land by the Mackintosh, the Camerons rallied 400 clansmen and marched into Badenoch, the territory of Clan Chattan, a confederation including the Mackintoshes, Davidsons, Macphersons, MacGillivrays, MacBeans and Farquharsons.

They arrived to find a battle already in progress between the Macphersons and the Davidsons over who should fight in the place of honour on the Mackintosh's right. The Mackintosh gave the place to the Davidsons, and the Macphersons, appalled, withdrew to watch the combat from across the Spey. With a furious charge the Camerons cut the Davidsons to pieces, and were set to finish off the Mackintoshes when the Macphersons at last joined in and put the Camerons to flight.

FAR RIGHT: *The Highland cattle that fed the clansmen were also a weapon in clan warfare – cattle-raiding became a method of reinforcing claims to land and of taking rent, whether it was owed or not.*

Inverary Castle, seat of the Duke of Argyll, the head of Clan Campbell.

THE ACQUISITIVE CAMPBELLS

James IV issued many of the chiefs with a 'sheepskin grant', a royal parchment deed emphasising that their properties were held directly from the crown. This attempt to reinforce feudalism was used to advantage by Campbell of Argyll, who also held a lease to several properties formerly held by the Lords of the Isles. Territorially acquisitive, the Campbells set about completely dominating the adjacent land. The MacGregors held land in Argyllshire and Perthshire on the clan principle, and the Campbells began to demand rents from them. As their lands were seized, the spirit of the MacGregor clansmen was broken, while their chief became a mere tenant of Campbell of Glenorchy. When, in 1570, the 10th MacGregor chief attempted to resist Campbell, he was captured and beheaded.

THE MACGREGORS ARE OUTLAWED

In 1603 the Campbell chief, the Earl of Argyll, saw a way to finish off the MacGregors for ever by encouraging a quarrel between the MacGregors and the Colquhouns of Luss. A 300-strong MacGregor force met 700 Colquhouns at Glenfruin. Splitting their force, the MacGregors attacked from two sides, slaughtering 140 Colquhouns.

James VI, about to leave for England to unite the two crowns, was furious at this bloodthirsty display of disunity, and before leaving Scotland he had the Privy Council outlaw the MacGregors. The MacGregor chief surrendered to Argyll in return for a promise of safe conduct to England, where he intended to plead his clan's case. To keep his promise, Argyll took MacGregor as far as Berwick, then brought him back to Edinburgh for execution.

Obedience to the King

THE only time a substantial group of clans would combine was in support of the Stuart dynasty. It was strongly felt that the Stuart monarch was the Chief of Chiefs – yet when the Stuarts took an interest in the clans, their aim was to make the Highlands conform with the Lowlands.

ABOVE: *Mulroy, the last clan battle, was the first conflict in which broadswords such as this were used almost exclusively by both sides.*

RIGHT: *Duntulm Castle in the Isle of Skye, stronghold of the MacDonalds of Sleat.*

DESPERATE MEASURES

James VI/I, weary of hearing about blood feuds and disputes, commissioned Lord Ochiltree to establish the rule of law in the Isles. A number of chiefs – Maclean of Duart, Donald Gorm of Sleat, Clanranald, MacLeod and Maclean of Ardgour – were invited aboard Lord Ochiltree's flagship to hear Andrew Knox, Bishop of the Isles, preach. Once the chiefs were aboard, however, the ship sailed for Edinburgh where they were imprisoned and only released when they agreed to support Knox in a policy of reforming the Isles.

In 1609 nine chiefs met at Iona and signed the Band and Statutes of Icolmkill, the so-called 'Statutes of Iona'. The intention was to spread 'civilisation' among the clans.

The Statutes of Iona

The Statutes demanded obedience to the king, ensured Lowland education for the sons of the gentry, abolished firearms and handfasting (a pagan marriage ceremony practised by the clansmen) and called for the discouragement of drinking and bards – presumably on the grounds that the two went together.

LEFT: *Eilean Donan Castle, the seat of Clan MacKenzie, originally built in 1220.*

THE MACDONALDS ARE BROUGHT TO HEEL

In response to the unexpected MacDonald victory, and because a crown officer had been killed in the skirmish, regular soldiers were sent to destroy the Keppoch lands and that branch of Clan Donald. The MacDonalds promptly joined Viscount Dundee, fighting superbly for the Stuart cause in the first of the Jacobite wars; but when 'Bonnie' Dundee died at Killicrankie, the deposed James VII/II unwisely replaced him with a regular officer, whose lack of understanding of the Highlanders lost him the respect of such vigorous men as Cameron of Lochiel and MacDonald of Sleat. Within a few days of his appointment, they went home.

THE FINAL BATTLE

The tradition of strife in the Highlands did not disappear immediately, however. It was not until 1688 that the last clan battle of all took place at Mulroy between the Mackintoshes and the MacDonalds of Keppoch. The MacDonalds held lands in Lochaber (Glen Spean and Glen Roy) on the clan principle, but the Mackintosh insisted he had crown permission – sheepskin grants – to hold the land. MacDonald scorned such legalities.

Sensing trouble, the Mackintosh got royal permission to attack the MacDonalds of Keppoch with an army of his own clansmen, his allies, and a company of royal troops under MacKenzie of Suddie. To meet this force, several sects of Clan Donald united, and annihilated the Mackintoshes at Mulroy.

Taming the Highlanders

WHEN James lost to William of Orange at the Battle of the Boyne in 1689 and fled to France, Britain was set to enter a new constitutional and commercially prosperous era in which there was no place for the clans. That, at least, was William III's point of view.

TAKING THE OATH

William decided that something drastic must be done about the Highlanders who had taken the side of the Stuarts. A scheme to buy loyalty from the clan chiefs proved ineffective, and it was decided that they should all take an oath of allegiance to William, not later than 1 January 1692. Those who refused would be met 'by fire and sword and all manner of hostility'.

The date was chosen with care, for the harsh Highland winter would partly immobilise the clansmen. Not surprisingly, the clan chiefs took the oath, and by 1 January only the powerful MacDonell of Glengarry and old MacIan MacDonald of Glencoe had defaulted.

ABOVE AND RIGHT: *The Pass of Glencoe. The Glencoe Massacre took place in harsh winter conditions, when escape was almost impossible.*

GLENCOE HOSPITALITY

MacIan tried to make his submission at Fort William on 31 December but, in the absence of a magistrate, was forced to go to Inverary, arriving there two days later. The sheriff-deputy was away, and MacIan was unable to take the oath until 6 January. At last William could make an example of someone.

Under the command of Captain Robert Campbell of Glenlyon, 120 men from the Earl of Argyll's Regiment of Foot went to Glencoe to be billeted in the cottages there. The troops were received with the legendary Highland courtesy, and for 15 days they shared friendship, food and drink with the Glencoe MacDonalds. Then on 12 February 1692 the Captain received an order authorising the massacre of the MacDonalds of Glencoe.

THE GLENCOE MASSACRE

The slaughter was to begin at 5 a.m. on 13 February. As the long dark night gave way to morning, the soldiers began their work. MacIan was shot in his bed and his wife had her rings wrenched from her fingers. Then 39 clansmen were attacked in their sleep, bound hand and foot, and murdered in the snow. Their cottages were set on fire as fresh snow began to fall. Other clansmen ran towards the caves, but many died in the snow; only about half the clan survived. This was not only a hideous crime, but also a deliberate mockery of the Highland tradition whereby hospitality was offered even to an enemy.

The Jacobite Uprisings

I N 1707 the parliaments of Scotland and England united. The clans resented their new status as minority groups in 'North Britain', and when the Hanoverian king George I came to the throne in 1714, it seemed the right moment to fight for the restoration of James Stuart, 'the Old Pretender', who lived in France.

THE INDECISIVE BATTLE OF SHERIFFMUIR

In 1715 the Earl of Mar, as leader of the Jacobites, summoned the clan chiefs to a grand hunt at Braemar, where he raised the Standard for James VIII/III, and announced himself to be the Commander-in-Chief of Scotland.

Mar had the support of most of the Highland chiefs, but his military incompetence squandered this potential strength. With around 10,000 clansmen Mar took Perth, and he could have taken Stirling and pressed on to Edinburgh had he not been intimidated by the Duke of Argyll's reputation. In November he decided to march to Auchterarder, but by then Argyll was ready to take on the Jacobites.

At Sheriffmuir the two sides met. Mar's Highlanders performed magnificently against Argyll's men, but what Mar lacked in tactical expertise Argyll had in abundance, and the conflict was indecisive.

RIGHT: *The Black Watch Monument at Aberfeldy pays tribute to General George Wade's military policy force, made up of men from six companies commanded by Lord Lovat, Grant of Ballindalloch, Munro of Culcairn and three Campbells.*

FAR RIGHT: *Wade's Bridge at Aberfeldy, built in 1733, was one of a number of bridges and roads constructed between 1726 and 1737 to open up the Highlands.*

TAKING THE CONSEQUENCES

After the battle the Jacobite clans grabbed what booty they could and made off home with it. At the prospect of another battle with Argyll (and more booty), the clans rallied again early in 1716. Mar, however, settled for retreat and, tired of their leader's procrastination, the clans deserted. James Francis Edward had the same idea – a month after landing at Peterhead he had seen enough, and left Scotland for France with Mar. After the collapse of the rebellion, the Highlanders were left to take the consequences.

LEFT: *The Old Pretender, James Francis Edward Stuart (1688–1766), son of James VII/III, exiled in 1689. The term 'Jacobite' comes from the Latin* Jacobus *for James.*

WADE'S REFORMS

The impenetrable Highlands were at last opened up by General George Wade, Scotland's Commander-in-Chief, with a network of new roads and bridges built between 1726 and 1737. Under the Disarming Act, Wade deprived the clans of many weapons. Lastly, he reorganised the six Highland Independent Companies to police the Highlands.

In 1724 General Wade estimated that there were around 22,000 men capable of bearing arms – of whom more than half would be likely to support a Stuart rebellion. What the government feared, therefore, was not the quantity of the opposition, but the quality of their fighting.

'Their Notions of Virtue and Vice are very different from the more civilised part of Mankind. They think it a most Sublime Virtue to pay Servile and Abject Obedience to the Commands of the Chieftains, altho' in opposition to their Sovereign and the Laws of their Kingdom, and to encourage this, their Fidelity, they are treated by their Chiefs with great Familiarity, they partake with them in their Diversions, and shake them by the Hand wherever they meet them.'

GENERAL GEORGE WADE'S REPORT TO THE GOVERNMENT ON THE HIGHLANDERS, 1724

The Evolution of Highland Dress

T HE word 'tartan' comes from the French *tiretaine* and Spanish *tiritana*, used to describe a coloured woollen material. In Gaelic the word is *breacan*, and was originally applied to an expansive chequered blanket, which was skilfully developed by the Celts of Scotland, eventually becoming the national dress of their country.

BELOW: *A detail from a portrait by J. Michael Wright of Sir Mungo Murray, a 17th-century Highland chieftain. The belted plaid is worn with Restoration doublet and the traditional arms of the Highlander – pistol, dirk, broadsword and long musket.*

The Plaid itself gives pleasure to the sight,
To see how all its sets imbibe the light;
Forming some way, which even to me lies hid,
White, black, blue, yellow, purple, green, and red.
Let Newton's royal club thro' prisms stare,
To view celestial dyes with curious care,
I'll please myself, nor shall my sight ask aid
Of crystal gimcracks to survey the plaid.

TARTANA, *ALLAN RAMSAY, 1686–1758*

RIGHT: *The Baird tartan, from the Old Scottish* baird, *meaning to dress very richly.*

The Scottish Highlander began to wear the *breacan feile*, or belted plaid, around the end of the 16th century. It consisted of about five yards of double tartan pleated and fastened round the waist by a belt so that the lower half formed a kilt and the upper half, pinned at the left shoulder with a brooch, hung down as a plaid. This left the arms free for work or war, or it could be used as a blanket if the Highlander had to spend a night out in the open.

The belted plaid was the everyday all-weather dress of the ordinary clansman. The Highland nobility favoured instead the skintight breeches known as trews, which were especially prized because of the considerable skill needed to match the tartan sett.

During the 17th century the familiar *feile beag*, or little kilt, appeared. It was derived from the kilt part of the *breacan feile*, and consisted of five yards of single tartan whose sewn pleats were fastened round the waist with a strap. The little kilt probably had economic attractions for the poorer clansmen, who would find the belted plaid too expensive. It would also have prevented their indecent exposure when they threw off their belted plaids for battle.

The wearing of tartan was given a huge boost by the parliamentary Union of 1707, which reduced Scotland effectively to the level of a province. Suddenly the tartan became a national symbol of patriotic disapproval of the Union, until disaster for the clans and their distinctive Highland dress came in 1745 in the shape of Bonnie Prince Charlie.

RIGHT: *'A Highland Man', from John Speed's map of Scotland in the late 16th/early 17th century, showing an early stage in the evolution of the belted plaid.*

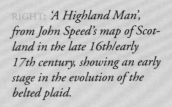

Tartan Hues

The first tartans were simple checks coloured with vegetable dyes. They were made by locals for locals, and became district tartans as a rough guide to a Highlander's geographical base. Later they developed to combine the Highlander's love of colour with a more practical need for camouflage.

Brooch to fasten plaid

Long shoulder plaid

Dirk

Sporran

Battledress blouse

Basket-hilted broadsword

Plain hose for day wear

Low shoe with buckle

The Battle of Culloden

THIRTY years after his father's failure in the '15 uprising, Charles Louis Philip Casimir Stuart landed at Eriskay – a tiny Hebridean island – with seven followers and no armed support. He had come to a country he knew nothing of, to take a crown he had never seen. Bonnie Prince Charlie 'threw himself upon the mercy of his countrymen, rather like a hero of romance than a calculating politician'.

RIGHT: *The Glenfinnan Memorial at the head of Loch Shiel. The column was erected in 1815 by Alexander MacDonald of Glenaladale, descendant of a devoted Jacobite.*

THE YOUNG PRETENDER

When MacDonald of Boisdale told him to go home, Charles said, 'I am come home.' He then predicted that 'my faithful Highlanders will stand by me'. With naïve confidence in the justice of his cause, Charles won the astute Cameron of Lochiel to his side and on 19 August 1745 raised his Standard at Glenfinnan before some 1,200 clansmen. From here he went from strength to strength, first taking Edinburgh and then spectacularly defeating Sir John Cope at Prestonpans. Bonnie Prince Charlie was in command of all Scotland. That was not, however, enough for a Stuart.

LEFT: *Detail from a portrait of Bonnie Prince Charlie dressed in red tartan, and wearing the Star and Ribbon of the Garter. The white cockade on his bonnet is the symbol of the House of Stuart.*

The Highland Charge

The Highland Charge depended on sheer recklessness to terrorise the enemy. Advancing three deep, the Highlanders would break into small units led by chieftains, rush forward firing pistols, then draw their broadswords and slash into the enemy. The technique was used with great success by Bonnie Prince Charlie until the Battle of Culloden, when the charge of the exhausted Highlanders was easily absorbed by the Hanoverians, seen here in David Morier's painting.

BELOW RIGHT: *The Culloden Memorial Cairn, erected in 1881 by Duncan Forbes, the 10th Laird of Culloden, marks the battlefield.*

DEFEATED BY 'THE BUTCHER'

With his 5,000-strong Highland army, Charles marched into England, taking Carlisle, Preston, Lancaster, Manchester, Macclesfield and then Derby.

Suddenly, within only 150 miles of London, the Prince's advisers began to panic, realising they faced an army some six times larger than their own. The Prince wanted to go on. He had known only victory so far and reasoned that he had an excellent chance of success; but caution prevailed, and the Highland army retreated, as far as Inverness. Then at Culloden, on 16 April 1746, the exhausted, starving, ill-equipped Highland army was attacked by 9,000 regular troops commanded by the Duke of Cumberland. Although he had never won a battle before, it took Cumberland just 25 minutes to destroy the Highland army. He could hardly have failed: the Highlanders had rations of one biscuit apiece and had just taken part in a disorganised night march. They were in no condition to do battle.

BROKEN SPIRITS

Cumberland, 'the Butcher', showed no mercy. The wounded were left to die, the captured were burned alive and mutilated, and the dead were left to rot, while any villages and towns Cumberland felt were sympathetic to Jacobitism were destroyed. The Prince escaped, became a fugitive in the Hebrides, and later returned to Europe to a pathetic life of debauchery.

The Highlanders were crushed. Their spirit was finally broken with a new Disarming Act, a ban on Highland dress, and a planned campaign to discourage the Gaelic tongue and make the clansmen God-fearing Protestant folk.

17

A Lasting Pride

I**T** may seem strange that Lowland Scotland could rejoice over the extermination of the Highland way of life, but rejoice it did. Scotland was two nations – one commercially minded in motivation and English in sympathy, the other agricultural and Gaelic in temperament. And yet no sooner was the English-speaking world rid of the clans than it wanted to preserve their memory. It wanted the picturesque costumes without the Gaelic-speaking barbarian inside them.

ABOVE RIGHT: *The Atholl Highlanders at Blair Castle, the only private army in Britain, headed by the Duke of Atholl. In 1745 Blair was the last private castle in Britain to be besieged.*

THE CROWN EMBRACES THE HIGHLANDERS

In 1822 George IV visited Edinburgh, clad in kilt and plaid in the Stuart tartan. After a dinner in Parliament House, George proposed a toast: 'Health to the chieftains and clans, and God Almighty bless the Land of Cakes. Drink this with three times three, gentlemen.'

In later years, Queen Victoria and her consort Prince Albert made a museum out of their Scotophilia. After holidaying with Victoria at Balmoral, Albert bought the estate, replacing the old castle with a grandiose new castle which he personally supervised, right down to the tartan carpets. Victoria could never exhaust Balmoral's charms, or the historical associations of the Highlands. After visiting the Glenfinnan monument in 1873, the Queen wrote: 'What a scene it must have been in 1745! And here was I, descendant of the Stuarts and of the very king whom Prince Charles sought to overthrow, sitting and walking about quite privately and peaceably.'

ABOVE: *The Clan Donald Centre, Skye, one of many centres and museums set up around the country to celebrate the existence of the clans.*

A TRADITION SURVIVES

It was true. The clans had been tamed out of existence, and only survived in memory. Yet it is a powerful memory that makes everyone with Scottish connections long to be affiliated to a clan. Today there are almost a thousand pipe bands in Scotland, and more than a thousand tartans (though most of them would have baffled the clansmen!). Clan societies preserve old castles, international clan-gatherings are held, visitors constantly seek evidence in the straths and glens that the clans really were what we believe them to have been.

At the time of the clans' defeat, they were an anachronism in terms of Lowland economic and social organisation. But they had a language and a culture and a landscape of their own, things that were taken from them. Perhaps it is their exit from history – so dramatically total, so tragically sudden – that makes people feel so sentimental towards the clans today.

LEFT: *Balmoral Castle, Grampian, described by Queen Victoria as her 'dear paradise'.*

Proscription and Revival

WHEN the 1747 Act for the 'Abolition and Proscription of the Highland Dress' was first passed, the troops were ordered to 'kill upon the spot any person dressed in the Highland garb' – even in the remote areas of the Highlands, where people had neither access to information about Acts of Parliament, nor the financial means to acquire a new outfit.

BELOW: The manufacture of tartan cloth, once a cottage craft practised all over Scotland, is now a fully mechanised operation carried out in mills in the Scottish Borders.

The Abolition of Highland Dress

'No man or boy within that part of Great called Scotland, other than such as shall be employed as Officers and Soldiers in His Majesty's Forces, shall, on any pretext whatsoever, wear or put on the clothes commonly called Highland clothes … the Plaid, Philabeg, or little Kilt, Trowse, Shoulder-belts, or any part whatsoever of what peculiarly belongs to the Highland garb; and that no tartan or party-coloured plaid or stuff shall be used for Great Coats or Upper Coats.'

Active persecution of Highland dress virtually stopped, however, when George III came to the throne in 1760. George was fascinated by the romance of the Stuarts and had, in his Scottish Prime Minister Lord Bute, a man well aware of the hostility created by the existence of the Dress Proscription Act. The Highland Society of London, founded in 1778, appointed a committee to fight for the repeal of the Act, and in 1782 the repeal Bill passed unopposed through both Houses of Parliament.

LEFT AND BELOW: Tartans are sported at the traditional Highland gatherings when clan members get together to enjoy Scottish games, music and competitions.

The Gaelic proclamation circulated to announce the repeal began: 'Listen, Men! This is bringing before all the Sons of the Gael that the King and Parliament of Britain have for ever abolished the Act against the Highland Dress … This must bring great joy to every Highland heart. You are no longer bound down to the unmanly dress of the Lowlander.' However, in the 35 years that the ban had been in force many 'Sons of the Gael' had been cleared out of their homes or had emigrated. Highland dress did not immediately revive.

It was the great novelist Sir Walter Scott who put tartan back on the map of Scotland. In 1822 he persuaded George IV to visit Scotland – the first reigning monarch to do so since Charles II – and to appear in kilt and plaid, and let the Highland gentry know that they would be expected to do likewise. George IV revelled in the occasion, and the tartan industry was born out of his visit. The firm of William Wilson & Son of Bannockburn, whose list of tartans had been quite insignificant in 1800, manufactured about 150 at the time of the royal visit. In 1842 *Vestiarium Scoticum* was published, an impressive, if not wholly authentic, catalogue of tartans. Tartan was here to stay, for both Highlanders and Lowlanders – the following pages show a selection of modern clans and their tartans.

Bagpipe Making

The bag is made of very soft sheepskin or sealskin, and must keep air in and moisture out. Five stocks – short, heavy wooden tubes – are tied into the bag. The three drones, the blowpipe and the chanter are pushed firmly into the stocks. Finally, the pipes are sealed (or hemped) with yellow hemp to prevent any air from escaping where two pieces of wood join.

ALASTAIR MACDONELL OF GLENGARRY
(1771–1828)

Colonel Macdonell, with his high-necked tunic, ivory-handled dirk and decorative sporran, may have been the original of Fergus Mac-Ivor in Sir Walter Scott's *Waverley*. Scott's romantic portrayal of the clans did much to promote the modern clan movement.

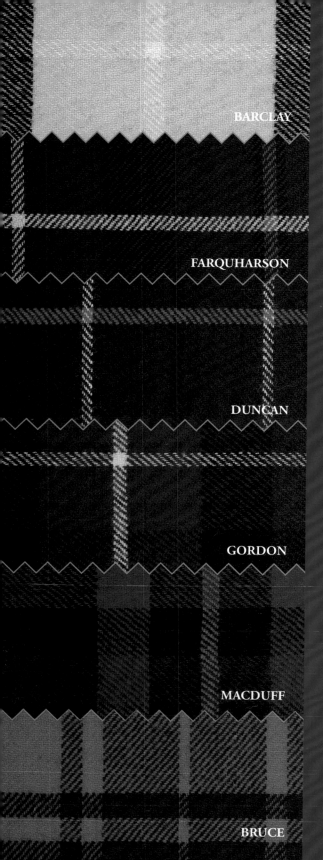

BARCLAY

FARQUHARSON

DUNCAN

GORDON

MACDUFF

BRUCE

The Cairngorms & East Coast

BARCLAY, from the Berkeleys who came to England with William the Conqueror. The Barclays have lands in Kincardineshire and Aberdeenshire. Motto AUT AGERE AUT MORI *Either action or death*

FARQUHARSON, from Gaelic *MacFhearchair*, meaning 'Son of the very dear one'. Clan Farquharson lands are in Aberdeenshire and Invercauld. Motto FIDE ET FORTITUDINE *By fidelity and fortitude*

DUNCAN, from Gaelic *Donnachaidh* meaning 'Brown warriors'. Duncan lands are in Atholl and Lundie in Fife. Motto DISCE PATI *Learn to suffer*

GORDON, from the parish of Gordon in Berwickshire. The Gordons went from the Lowlands to Aberdeenshire in the 14th century. Their lands are in Strathbogie, Deeside and the environs of Aberdeen. Motto BYDAND *Remaining* Pipe Music *The Gordon's March*

MACDUFF, from Gaelic *Mac-Dubh*, meaning 'Son of the dark one'. The Macduff lands are in Fife, Lothian, Strathbran and Strathbogie. Motto DEUS JUVAT *God assists*

BRUCE, named after Robert de Brus, a French knight from Brix and an ancestor of the Scottish king Robert the Bruce. The Bruce lands are in Annandale, Clackmannan and Elgin. Motto FUIMUS *We have been*

Northern Scotland

SINCLAIR, from the French parish of Saint-Clair-sur-Elle in Normandy. The clan's lands are in Midlothian, Orkney and Caithness.
Motto COMMIT THY WORK TO GOD
Pipe Music *The Sinclair's March (Spaidsearachd Mhic nan Cearda)*

MACKENZIE, from Gaelic *MacCoinnich*, meaning 'Son of the fair'. MacKenzie lands are in Ross and Cromarty, and the Isle of Lewis.
Motto LUCEO NOR URO *I shine, not burn*
Pipe Music *Caber Féidh*

SUTHERLAND, from the district of the same name south of Caithness. The clan had associations with the Murrays. Their lands are in Sutherland.
Motto SANS PEUR *Without fear*
Pipe Music *The Earl of Sutherland's March*

ROSS, from Ross-shire, *ros* being Gaelic for head-land. The clan Andrias acquired the earldom of Ross *c.*1234, and changed their name. Clan Ross lands are in Rosshire, Ayrshire and Renfrewshire.
Motto SPEM SUCCESSUS ALIT
Success nourishes hope
Pipe Music *The Earl of Ross's March*

MACKAY, from Gaelic *MacAdoidh*, meaning 'Son of Aodh'. Their lands are in Ross and Sutherland, and Argyll.
Motto MANU FORTI *With a strong hand*
Pipe Music *Mackay's March*

GUNN of Kilernan, from Norse *gunn-arr*. The clan chiefs claimed descent from Gunni, Norse son of Olave the Black, King of Man and the Isles. Clan Gunn have lands in Caithness and Sunderland.
Motto AUT PAX AUT BELLUM
Either peace or war
Pipe Music *The Gunn's Salute*

SINCLAIR

MACKENZIE

SUTHERLAND

ROSS

MACKAY

GUNN OF KILERNAN

MACLEAN OF DUART

MACDONALD OF CLANRANALD

MACNEIL(L)

MACLEOD

MACDONALD

MACMILLAN

The Islands & West Coast

MACLEAN of Duart, meaning 'Son of Gillean'. Maclean have had associations with MacLaines of Lochbuie, MacDougalls of Lorn and MacDonalds, Lords of the Isles. Their lands are in Morven, Mull, Coll and Tiree.
Motto *Virtue mine honour*
Pipe Music *The Maclean's March*

MACDONALD of Clanranald, from MacDonald and Ranald, younger son of John, the first Lord of the Isles. Clanranald lands are in the Northern Isles and North-west Argyll.
Motto *My hope is constant in thee*
Pipe Music *Clanranald's March (Spaid searachd Mhic Mhic Ailein)*

MACNEIL(L), meaning 'Son of Niall', the Irish for 'champion'. MacNeil(l) lands are in Barra, Gigha, Knapdale and Colonsay.
This tartan is MacNeil of Barra.
Motto VINCERE VEL MORI *To conquer or die*
Pipe Music *MacNeil of Barra's March*

MACLEOD, from Leod, son of the 13th-century Olave the Black. The MacLeod lands are in Skye, Lewis and Harris.
Motto *Hold fast*
Pipe Music *MacLeod's Praise*

MACDONALD, from Gaelic *Domhnull*, meaning 'Water Ruler' and Donald, grandson of Somerled, King of the Isles. Clan Donald lands are in the Western Isles.
Motto PER MARE PER TERRAS *By sea and by land*
Pipe Music *March of the MacDonalds*

MACMILLAN, from Gaelic *MacMhaolain*, meaning 'Son of the tonsured one'. Macmillan lands are in Lochaber, Argyll and Galloway. This is Ancient Macmillan tartan.
Motto MISERIS SUCCERRERE DISCO
I learn to succour the distressed

The Central Highlands

CALEDONIA. There are several Caledonian tartans, which can be worn by those wishing to be associated with Scotland but not with a specific clan.

GRAHAM of Montrose, from Old English *graeham* meaning greyhome. Graham lands are in the Barony of Mugdock, north of Glasgow, Loch Katrine in the Trossachs, around Kincardine Castle in Perthshire, and around Dundee and Montrose.
Motto NE OUBLIE *Do not forget*
Pipe Music *Killiecrankie*

ROSE, from the Norman family de Rose. Their lands are in Strathnairn and Rosshire, and Kilravock Castle is still inhabited by the chief of the clan.
Motto *Constant and true*

CAMPBELL, from Gaelic *cam-beul*, meaning 'crooked mouth'. Clan Campbell lands are in Argyll, Cawdor, Loudon and Breadalbane.
This tartan belongs to Campbell of Argyll.
Motto NE OBLIVISCARIS *Forget not*
Pipe Music *The Campbells are coming (Baile Ionaraora)*

ROBERTSON, from Robert Riabbhach (Grizzled Robert) Duncanson, 4th chieftain of Clan Donnachaidh, from whom both the Robertsons and the Duncans were descended. Clan Robertson has lands in Struan.
Motto VIRTUTIS GLORIA MERCES
Glory is the reward of valour
Pipe Music *The Clan Donnachie have arrived (Teachd Chlann Donnachaidh)*

CAMERON, from Gaelic *Cam-shron*, meaning hook-nose. Clan Cameron lands are in Lochiel and Northern Argyll; Achnacarry Castle is still the home of the chief.
Motto AONAIBH RI CHEILE *Unite*
Pipe Music *Piobaireachd Dhonuill Duibh*

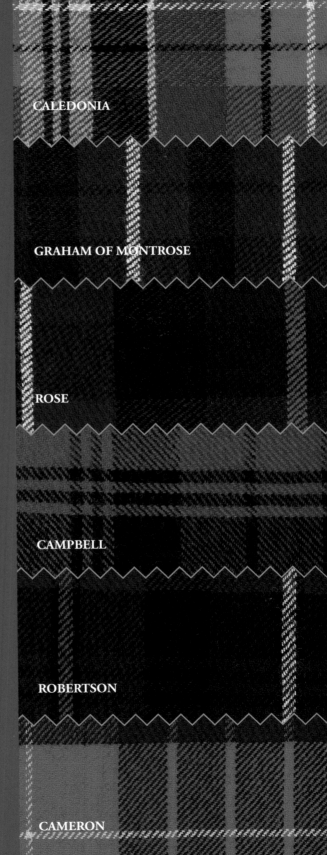

CALEDONIA

GRAHAM OF MONTROSE

ROSE

CAMPBELL

ROBERTSON

CAMERON

HAMILTON

MONTGOMERIE

MACGREGOR

LENNOX

ROYAL STEWART

WALLACE

Southern Highlands

HAMILTON, from the north-of-England town of Hameldone. The Hamilton family are the hereditary Keepers of Holyroodhouse and had lands in Renfrewshire and Arran.
Motto *Through* [sic]

MONTGOMERIE. Eglinton is the seat of the Montgomeries, later the earls of Eglinton.
The Montgomeries had lands in Eglinton, Ardrossan and Kintyre.
Motto GARDEZ BIEN *Look well*

MACGREGOR, from Gaelic *MacGrioghair*, meaning 'Son of Gregory'. The clan's motto refers to its descent from Grioger, son of King Alpin, in the 8th century. Clan lands are on the eastern border of Argyll and the western border of Perthshire.
Motto SRIOGHAL MO DHREAN *Royal is my race*
Pipe music *Chase of Glen Fruin*
(Ruaig Ghlinne Freoine)

LENNOX DISTRICT TARTAN, one of the oldest recorded. The surname Lennox is usually thought to show relation to Clans Stewart or MacFarlane, any of whom may choose to wear the ancient Lennox tartan.

ROYAL STEWART, from the 12th-century High Steward of Scotland whose descendant Walter married Marjory, daughter of Robert the Bruce; from them descended the Royal House of Stewart. Their lands are in Renfrewshire, Teviotdale and Lauderdale.
Motto VIVESCIT VULNERE VIRTUS
Courage grows strong at a wound

WALLACE, from the term *Wallensis*, used to designate the Britons of Strathclyde who were of the same stock as the Welsh. Sir William Wallace was Scotland's greatest patriot, refusing to recognise the sovereignty of Edward I. The Wallaces held lands in Ayrshire and Renfrewshire.
Motto PRO LIBETARTE *For liberty*

The Lowlands

KERR, possibly from Gaelic *cearr* meaning 'a place of strength' or 'fortress', or a Celtic word meaning 'strength'. Prominent in Border conflicts, the Kerr family had lands in Roxburghshire.
Motto SERO SED SERIO *Late but in earnest*

DOUGLAS, from Gaelic *Dubh-glas*, meaning 'black stream'. The history of the Douglases and of the Scottish throne are closely linked. Clan Douglas had lands in Lanarkshire, Galloway, Dumfriesshire and Angus.
Motto JAMAIS ARRIÈRE *Never behind*

SCOTT, from the Irish tribe, L.Scoti, which gave its name to Scotland. The Scotts were one of the most powerful border clans. Scott lands are in the Borders and Fife.
Motto AMO *I love*

FERGUSON, from the name of Fergus, Prince of Galloway, or King Fergus, founder of the Scottish kingdom that is now Argyll. Clan Ferguson had lands in Argyll, Perthshire, Dumfries, Galloway and the estate of Raith.
Motto DULCIUS EX ASPERIS
Sweeter after difficulties

ELLIOT, possibly from the town of Eliot in Forfarshire. Border clans were fierce and kept the law in their own way, and the Elliot clan was one of the largest and fiercest.
Motto FORTITER ET RECTE
With strength and right

JOHNSTON (or Johnstone), from Old English 'John's tun', meaning John's farm. The Johnstons were a warlike Border family remembered in Border song and story. They had lands in the Borders and Aberdeenshire.
Motto NUNQUAM NON PARATUS
Never unprepared

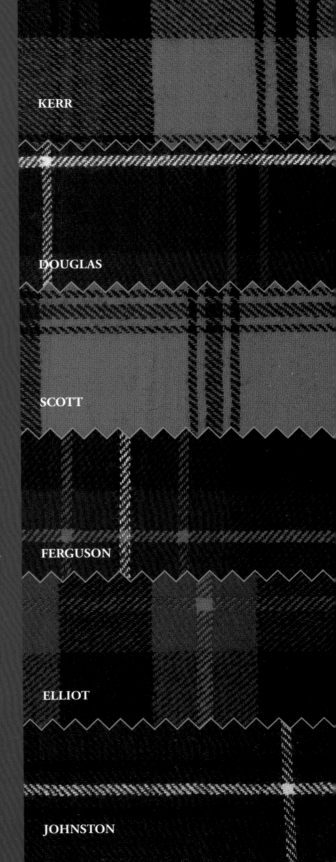

KERR

DOUGLAS

SCOTT

FERGUSON

ELLIOT

JOHNSTON

Some Clans & Septs and their Tartans

A CLAN is a collection of families who have a common ancestor and are subject to a single chieftain. A sept is a division of a clan. The tartans are in italic.

Abbot *Macnab*
Adam *Gordon*
Adamson *Mackintosh*
Alexander *MacAlister or MacDonell of Glengarry*
Allan *MacDonald of Clanranald or MacFarlane*
Allison *Allison*
Anderson *Anderson and Ross*
Andrew *Ross*
Angus *Angus and MacInnes*
Armstrong *Armstrong*
Arthur *MacArthur, Campbell or MacDonald*
Baillie *Baillie*
Bain, Bayne *MacBean, MacKay or Macnab*
Baird *Baird*
Barclay *Barclay*
Barrie *Dunbar, Farquharson or Gordon*
Bartholomew *Leslie or MacFarlane*
Baxter *Baxter and Macmillan*
Bell *Macmillan*
Berkeley *Barclay*
Black *Lamont, MacGregor or Maclean*
Boyd *Boyd and Stewart*
Brewer *Drummond or MacGregor*
Brodie *Brodie*
Brown *Lamont or Macmillan*
Bruce, Brus *Bruce*
Buchan *Buchan (Cumming)*
Buchanan *Buchanan*
Burnett *Burnett and Campbell*
Burns *Burns and Campbell*
Cairns *Ferguson or Grant*
Calder *Campbell of Cawdor*
Cameron *Cameron*
Campbell *Campbell, and Argyll, Breadalbane, Cawdor or Loudoun*
Carmichael *Carmichael, and MacDougall, Stewart of Appin or Stewart of Galloway*
Carnegie *Carnegie*
Chalmers *Cameron*
Chisholm *Chisholm*
Christie *Christie or Farquharson*
Clark, Clarkson, Clerk *Clark and Cameron, or Clan Chattan*
Cochrane *Cochrane and MacDonald*
Cockburn *Cockburn*
Collier *Robertson*
Colman *Buchanan*
Colquhoun *Colquhoun*
Cook *Stewart*
Coulson *MacDonald*
Cowan *Colquhoun or MacDougall*
Crawford *Crawford and Lindsay*
Cumming *Cumming*
Cunningham *Cunningham*
Currie *MacDonald or Macpherson*
Dalziel *Dalzell*
Davidson, Davie, Davis, Davison, Dawson *Davidson*
Dewar *Macnab or Menzies*
Donald, Donaldson *MacDonald*
Douglas *Douglas*
Dove *Buchanan*
Dow *Buchanan or Davidson*
Drummond *Drummond*
Duff *MacDuff*
Duffie, Duffy *Macfie*
Dunbar *Dunbar*
Duncan *Duncan and Robertson*
Dundas *Dundas*
Elder *Mackintosh*
Elliot *Elliot*

Erskine *Erskine*
Ewan, Ewen, Ewing *MacLachlan*
Farquhar *Farquharson*
Ferguson *Fergusson*
Findlay, Finlay *Farquharson*
Fleming *Murray*
Fletcher *Fletcher and MacGregor*
Forbes *Forbes*
Forsyth *Forsyth*
France *Stewart*
Fraser, Frazet *Fraser*
Fullarton, Fullerton *Stuart of Bute*
Galbraith *Galbraith and MacDonald, or MacFarlane*
Georgeson *Gunn*
Gibb, Gibson *Buchanan*
Gilbert, Gilbertson *Buchanan*
Gilchrist *MacLachlan or Ogilvy*
Gillespie *Macpherson*
Gilmore *Morrison*
Gilroy *Grant or MacGillivray*
Glen, Glennie *Mackintosh*
Gordon *Gordon*
Graeme, Graham *Graham (Menteith or Montrose)*
Grant *Grant*
Gray *Stewart of Atholl or Sutherland*
Gregor(y), Greig *MacGregor*
Gunn *Gunn*
Hamilton *Hamilton*
Hardie, Hardy *Farquharson or Mackintosh*
Harper *Buchanan*
Hawes *Campbell*
Hawthorn *MacDonald*
Hay *Hay*
Henderson *Henderson and Gunn, or MacDonald*
Home, Hume *Home*
Houston *MacDonald*
Hunter *Hunter*
Huntly *Huntly and Gordon*
Hutcheson, Hutchinson *MacDonald*
Inglis *Inglis*
Innes *Innes*
Irvine *Irvine*
Jameson, Jamieson *Gunn, Stuart of Bute*
Johnson *Gunn or MacDonald*
Johnston(e) *Johnstone*
Kay *Davidson*
Kean, Keene *Gunn or MacDonald*
Keith *Keith and Macpherson, or Sutherland*
Kellie, Kelly *MacDonald*
Kendrick *MacNaughton*
Kennedy *Kennedy and Cameron*
Kenneth *MacKenzie*
Kerr *Kerr*
Kilpatrick *Colquhoun*
King *Colquhoun or MacGregor*
Lamb *Lamont*
Lang *Leslie or MacDonald*
Laurence, Law *MacLaren*
Lennox *Lennox and MacFarlane, or Stewart*
Leslie *Leslie*
Lewis *MacLeod of Lewis*
Lindsay *Lindsay*
Livingstone *Livingstone, and Stewart of Appin or MacDougall*
Logan *Logan or MacLennan*
Low *MacLaren*
Lucas, Luke *Lamont*
Lumsden *Lumsden and Forbes*
Lyall *Sinclair*
Lyon *Farquharson or Lamont*
MacAdam *MacGregor*
MacAllister *MacAllister*